GREECE

A PICTURE BOOK TO REMEMBER HER BY

Designed by
DAVID GIBBON

Produced by
TED SMART

CRESCENT

INTRODUCTION

Greece has always been at the crossroads of history and the meeting place of East and West. Today it is the southern neighbour of Albania, Yugoslavia and Bulgaria and has a common land frontier in Thrace with European Turkey. The great sweep of the Greek islands begins in the Ionian Sea at Corfu which is about 110 kilometres from the heel of Italy, and continues south through Crete to within rowing distance of the Turkish coast at Kastellorizon in the east. Northwards the idyllic islands of the Cyclades, the Sporades and the Dodecanese reach out across the "wine-dark sea" of Homer's Aegean.

The sea has been a recurring theme in Greek history and culture from the fabulous voyages of Odysseus to the defeat of the Persian invaders by the Athenian navy at Mycale in 479 B.C. In modern times the battle of Navarino in 1827 was the precursor of the withdrawal of the Ottoman Turks and the creation of an independent Greece in 1830. Sea communications are particularly important in a country where land travel is impeded by mountainous terrain and where, except for part of the central mainland, the sea is within a range of about fifty kilometres. Today the Greek-owned merchant fleet is a major force in carrying the world's freight and of considerable economic importance to a country relatively poor in natural resources where in addition less than a quarter of the land can be cultivated. In Greece there are ever-present reminders of the past which even the most casual tourist ought not to overlook. "The Glory that was Greece" usually refers to the classical period of Athens around the fifth century B.C., typified by the Parthenon, but the older Minoan civilisation of Crete exerts a fascination which the reconstruction of the palace at Knossos has encouraged. The succeeding mainland civilisation at Mycenae in the Peloponnese from about 1400 B.C. had an influence which was felt as far afield as Egypt.

It is, of course, quite possible to visit Greece and not pay any attention to the monuments of the past if the lure of the sun and the beaches proves too strong. But the two are not incompatible as the major sites are outdoors, often in outstandingly beautiful settings. To visit Delphi – the "navel of the world" – is an unforgettable experience and may prompt one to wonder why Greece is the origin of so much that has endured in European civilisation. But it is not only in Europe that the legacy of Greece is to be found. The Greek city-state (the *polis*) went into decline following the defeat of Athens and Thebes by Philip of Macedon in 338 B.C. From then on the city-states became a part of an empire that Philip's son, Alexander, created in the Middle East after defeating Darius and taking over the Persian empire. At the time of his death in 323 B.C. Alexander's empire extended to India in the east and to Egypt in the south and although it split up after this the Greek culture persisted in the resulting kingdoms. Indeed it survived as the main civilising influence into the Roman empire of which Greece became a province and an educated Roman would have been familiar with Greek literature and culture. The recognition of Christianity as the official religion of the Roman empire by Constantine and the establishment of his new capital at Constantinople (A.D. 324-37) institutionalised Greek influence which persisted even when mainland Greece was invaded by the Huns from 447 and afterwards by the Slavs and the militant forces of Islam. When Byzantium fell to the Turks in 1453 it was felt to be the "last day" of Eastern Christendom but when Greece was then annexed as a province of the Ottoman empire it was the Orthodox church in Greece that preserved and fostered the cultural heritage in the difficult centuries of foreign occupation.

After the Napoleonic era the British acquired the Ionian islands whose improved economic circumstances assisted the subsequent revolt against the Turks which was publicised throughout Europe by the death of Lord Byron at the siege of Missolonghi in 1824. The story of Greece since the initial independence of the mainland south of Thessaly, together with some of the islands, in 1830 has been a turbulent succession of the ebbing and reviving fortunes of an alien monarchy, military dictatorships and hardship during World War II and the ensuing civil war. Today, after the interlude of the "Colonels' dictatorship", representative government is restored and Greece is an associate member of the European Economic Community, intent on increasing the prosperity of both the mainland and the islands. Tourism has helped considerably in this respect. A visitor to Greece will be aware of the evocative beauty and the dramatic contrasts of the landscape and the peculiarly brilliant quality of the light, as well as of the wild flowers in profusion and the superb fruit, olive oil, wine and fish. But the discerning will return home having also become aware of the ancient Hellas and Byzantium that lie behind modern Greece and maybe having heard, too, some of the footfalls across the centuries that reward the observant traveller in this intriguing land.

Left: Sunset at the Temple of Poseidon on Cape Sounion.

Thessaloniki (Salonika), on the north-east coast of Greece, is a city second only to Athens and the commercial capital of the north of the country. It was restored to Greece in October 1912 after centuries of Turkish occupation and the modern city *above left* is built round the ruins of the Greek, Roman and Byzantine Empires. The Arch of Galerius *left* is just such a ruin, it commemorates in marble reliefs the life of the Roman Emperor Galerius who ruled during the fourth century. The Rotunda of St. George *above* was built as a temple and has since been used as a church and a mosque. It is now a museum.

Overleaf: View from Pilion to Volos and the Gulf of Pagasae.

The Meteora in the mountains of central Greece is famous for its monasteries which date from the fourteenth century. They perch on pinnacles of rock *above, far right and overleaf.* Such sites were chosen by the monks for their inaccessibility and those wishing to visit them today have, in some cases, to climb ladders or ascend in baskets hauled up by the monks. Many of the original two dozen monasteries are now derelict. The monastery of Aghiou Stefanou *overleaf* has a superb view over the valley of Pinios.

Right: The picturesque fishing village of Afissos on the Gulf of Volos.

Delphi, built on the slopes of Mount Parnassus, was the spiritual and religious centre of ancient Greece. There is a lovely view from the Theatre over the Temple of Apollo to the valley below *left.* The Tholos *top* is a marble rotunda built during the fourth century B.C. The Treasury of the Athenians *above* was built to commemorate the victory over the Persians at Marathon in 490 B.C.

Overleaf: The hill village of Makrinitsa.

Athens is built on a small peninsula called Attica which juts out into the Aegean Sea. It probably first came into being as a fortress built on the rock of the Acropolis which is a steep crag dominating the surrounding plain. By the middle of the sixth century B.C. Athens had become the greatest city on the mainland of Greece and the Acropolis was crowned with temples. These early temples were destroyed during the wars with the Persians and the buildings which can be seen now *top left and far left* date from 480 B.C. The Propylaea *left* is the monumental gateway which forms the imposing entrance to the Acropolis. The Parthenon *above* is the crowning glory. It was built by the statesman Pericles between 447 and 432 B.C. The sculptor Phidias and the architect Ictinos directed the work and this, the "Great Temple" remains a monument to the genius of these three men.

The Temple of Victory *left* is an architectural masterpiece of classic Ionic simplicity which graces the south-west corner of the Acropolis. The Erechtheion *right* is the tomb of the legendary founder king of Athens. It was built between 421 and 406 B.C. on the ruins of an earlier temple destroyed when the Persians sacked the Acropolis in 480 B.C. The Porch of the Maidens forms a canopy over the Tomb of the King. One of the six original maidens is in the British Museum and the other five are also being replaced by copies and moved to a museum in Athens in order to protect them against further damage from atmospheric pollution. Recent measures have resulted in a dramatic reduction of atmospheric pollution which was threatening all of Athens' ancient buildings.

Below: The Acropolis floodlit at night.

Modern Athens is built around and over the ruins of the ancient city. The Central Food Markets straggle over an area of perhaps two square kilometres. Here fruit *top far left*, chicken *bottom near left* and meat *below* as well as many other foods may be bought. The sponge seller *left* was photographed in Constitution Square. Greece is one of the few remaining countries which still has divers who seek living sponges far beneath the sea.

Other street sights include *far left* the sandal-maker, and corn-on-the-cob roasted on braziers as here in Monastiraki Square. Orthodox priests may be seen chatting quietly as bustling city life carries on around them. Tourists in Athens are often puzzled by men who carry long wooden sticks covered in slips of paper *right*. They sell tickets for the weekly State Lottery.

The monuments of the ancient city are never far from everyday life in modern Athens and the courts of the Athens Tennis Club *bottom right* are over-shadowed by the towering columns of the Sanctuary of the Olympian Zeus.

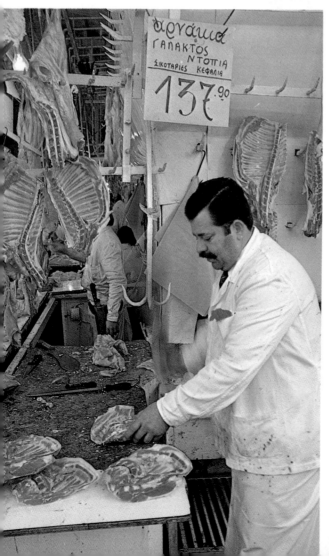

The Agora *left* lies below the Acropolis rock and was the heart of ancient Athens and the centre of the public life of the city. The octagonal Tower of the Winds *far left* is thought to have been erected in the first century B.C. It takes its name from the eight sculptured reliefs which depict the winds which blow from the eight points of the compass but it was, in fact, a remarkable water clock with a mechanism which regulated water passing through a cylinder, so marking the passage of the hours.

The white marble Olympic stadium *centre* was built in 1895 by George Averoff, a wealthy Greek from Alexandria, for the first modern Olympic Games which were held in 1896. The modern stadium is built on the site of the ancient Panathenaic Stadium and seats 70,000 spectators. The Greek Parliament Building *bottom right* dominates Constitution Square in the city centre. It was originally built as a residence for King Otto, the first king of modern Greece, from 1834-8, and is still often referred to as the "Old Palace". It now houses the Greek Parliament and the Council of State. The Tomb of the Unknown Soldier is also in Constitution Square; the Presidential (formerly Royal) Guards (Evzones) in their picturesque uniform and "pom-pom" shoes are on duty there twenty-four hours a day *right*.

The modern city of Athens sprawls nearly to Piraeus, the old harbour from which the ancient fleets once sailed. The Aegean Sea offers one of the loveliest cruising grounds in the Mediterranean and boats from all over Europe as well as from further afield cram the marinas and harbours close to Piraeus. The small harbour of Mikrolimani *below,* known locally as Turkolimano or Turkish Harbour, is used by racing yachts and dinghies and is the home of the Yacht Club of Greece. Fishermen *left* go out from the harbour which is surrounded by picturesque fish restaurants *top right* making it a popular place for dining out. This is a view of the harbour and restaurants as seen from the Yacht Club *bottom right.*

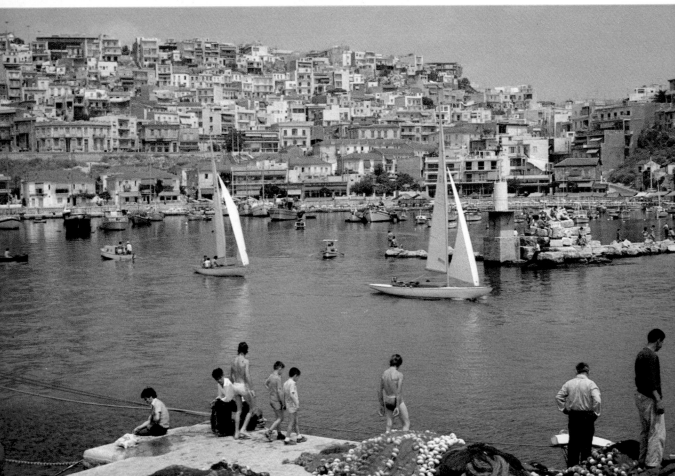

Crowded beaches and marinas edge the coast road out of Athens; Glyfada *top left and above* is one of the many popular resorts in Attica which are within easy reach of the city. Farther along the coast road, about sixty kilometres from Athens, the beautiful Doric temple, sacred to Poseidon, stands high on the promontory of Cape Sounion *right and far right* where it has been a landmark for nearly 2,500 years and is still used by sailors as they make their final approach to the Saronic Gulf and to Athens.

The six kilometres long Corinth canal cuts through the narrow isthmus of Corinth linking the Aegean Sea with the Gulf of Corinth and thence with the Adriatic and Italy. The idea of cutting a canal through this narrow land bridge which links central and northern Greece with the Peloponnese, thus saving ships the long and often arduous journey south around Cape Matapan, was a very old one. The ancient Greeks planned a canal; so did the Romans. The existing canal was built by a French company between 1882 and 1893; a car ferry in the canal *left* and a view through the canal from the deck of a ship *right* showing one of the two bridges which link the two sections of mainland Greece. Such a narrow isthmus is obviously of great strategic importance. The heights of Acrocorinth were first fortified as early as the seventh century B.C. and were used as a refuge by the Corinthians in times of trouble. The fortress was taken and retaken, fortified and refortified throughout the centuries, by all who hoped to dominate the Peloponnese. The Slavs and Bulgarians, Franks, Venetians and Turks, among others, left their mark here and have made it one of the most fascinating fortresses in Greece; it has a superb view across the ancient city to modern Corinth and the shores of the Gulf *below*.

The Temple of Apollo *above* at ancient Corinth is one of the oldest in Greece, dating from between 550 and 525 B.C. Seven of the Doric columns still stand supporting fragments of architrave. There are extensive ruins at the site of the old city which was on the plateau dominating the eastern end of the Gulf of Corinth. Epidaurus, south of Corinth, is another ruined city. It is famous for its superb early theatre *right* and a festival of Greek plays is held here each summer.

Mycenae was the home of
Agamemnon, the legendary king of
Mycenae and Argos. The city was
destroyed in 470 B.C. but the ruins can
still be seen *above and right*. The
civilisation based on Mycenae was an
important one dating from about 2000
B.C. Excavations of the great fort have
produced ornaments and jewellery
made of pure gold and bowls
beautifully engraved with stories from
the legends. Nafplion *far right* is
almost due south of Corinth, but also
lies on the coast, on the Gulf of Argos.
It was the seat of the first modern
Greek government after the War of
Independence of 1821, before Athens
was liberated from Turkish rule.

Pylos *above*, formerly called Navarino, is a
port on the south-west of the Peloponnese
off which, in 1827, the fleets of Britain,
France and Russia combined and defeated
the Turkish navy and so ensured the
independence of Greece.

Greece is a country of high mountains
and rocky coasts; the one is never very far
from the other. This is a mountainous area
of the Peloponnese near Leonidion village
left; Monastery Elenis is also near
Leonidion *top left.*

Olives and olive oil are an important
part of Greek agriculture and provide one
of the major exports. The olive tree is often
so valuable to the farmer that it forms part
of a woman's dowry. The trees are
painstakingly pruned and the olives are
gathered carefully by hand *far left.*

Mistra was the capital of Byzantine Greece and from what remains today we can see what a fourteenth century Byzantine town looked like; these are some of the ruins *bottom left*. It was situated on a commanding hill near the ancient city of Sparta and was ceded to the Byzantine Empire as ransom in 1259. It was taken by the Turks in 1460; the Venetians ruled from 1687–1715 when it again came under Turkish domination. In 1770 the town was burnt by the Albanians during a Greek revolt against the Ottomans. Mistra is famous for its delightful Byzantine churches and monasteries, such as the monastery *left*, which contain particularly beautiful and elegant wall paintings.

Below: A mountain road in the Peloponnese.

Olympia in the western Peloponnese was the site *left* of the ancient Olympic games. Every four years from 776 B.C. athletes, authors, poets, artists and sculptors met to take part in a great festival at the temple of Zeus. Later the festival became an expression of the Greek ideal that a man's body should be as fit and healthy as his mind. In A.D. 393 the games were abolished by the Roman emperor Theodosius and were not revived until 1896. There is now a modern academy *above* on the site of the ancient games.

Faces of Greece

Today a living relic of Byzantium can be seen at Mount Athos – the Holy Mountain – which is a self-governing republic of twenty sovereign monasteries under Greek protection situated at the most northerly of the three peninsulas south-east of Thessaloniki. Tradition has it that the Virgin Mary landed at Athos with St. John, having been blown off course when sailing to visit Lazarus in Cyprus. Out of deference to the Visitor no other females have been allowed on Athos ever since. The oldest monastery still in existence, the Great Lavra, was founded in 963. Pantocratoros *left* is on the northern coast of the peninsula. Farther west on the same coastline lies Vatopedi. The chapel *below* is nearby. On the south coast of the peninsula, the monastery of Dionysiou *right* is built on rock rising straight out of the sea.

Overleaf: The harbour at Skiathos, the island capital of the Sporades group.

Corfu is the most important of the Ionian Islands to the north-west of Greece, and has been a popular tourist centre for many years. The first sight the traveller has of the island as he approaches from the sea is often a hazy one *bottom right*. There are picturesque and secluded coves like this one at Sidari on the north coast *above*, and lovely views like this one from Kanoni point looking south to the charming convent of Vlaherna with the tiny island of Pontikonissi (Mouse Island) behind *top right*.

The town of Corfu, capital of the islands, reflects a past dominated by the Venetians who occupied the Ionian Islands from 1386 until they were ceded to the French during the Napoleonic Wars. They then passed to the Turks, the Russians and the French and finally to Great Britain after the defeat of Napoleon. Under Queen Victoria the islands were restored to Greece in 1864.

The ancient port of Piraeus is now the maritime centre of Greece, a modern commercial harbour crowded with liners, cargo ships and island ferries *above*. Although a few of the Aegean islands can now be reached by air, most still depend entirely on the inter-island ferries which ply back and forth from Piraeus. From Piraeus the Saronic Gulf *left* leads to the nearer Islands of Aegina, Hydra *top right* and Poros *bottom right*. Hydra was a considerable maritime power in the eighteenth and nineteenth centuries and was the base of the powerful naval fleet which won many victories against the Turks in the 1821 War of Independence. The beautiful old town is built on the steep rocky slopes around the harbour which is now filled with fishing boats and pleasure yachts. It attracts artists and writers and the waterfront is lined with craft shops and boutiques.

The island of Poros is separated from the mainland by a narrow channel through which the island steamers pass. The picturesque town of whitewashed houses and steep, narrow, vine-shaded paths climbs up and over a hill by the edge of the channel. There is a large, sheltered bay, dotted with tiny islands and surrounded by pine-fringed coves and beaches, which provides an ideal cruising ground for dinghy and small boat sailors.

Tinos is an island of the Cyclades group. The village of Pyrgos *left* is famous for the number of sculptors it has produced. Marble has been quarried from the nearby mountains since ancient times and has been used for some of the loveliest sculpture in Greece. The village is a showplace of the art; every building is embellished with marble doorways, columns and arches and even the smallest houses have marble reliefs set in their whitewashed walls.

Syros *below* is the capital of the Cyclades; it was once an important port on the Mediterranean shipping routes but since the last war the island's economy has declined although a modern ship-building and repair yard equipped with floating docks still operates.

Right; A windmill on Mykonos at sunset.

Of all the sun-drenched islands in the Aegean Sea, Mykonos is probably the most famous. It is a treeless, rocky but strangely fertile island in the centre of the Cyclades. The narrow streets of the town of Mykonos *right,* where even the paving stones are ringed with whitewash, have white flat-roofed houses on either side, made colourful with painted balconies. Near the water's edge the houses rise straight from the sea *above,* giving this area the nickname 'Little Venice'. The atmosphere is gay, with music-making beside the harbour in the sunshine *left;* the instruments are a fiddle and a bouzouki.

Fishing on Mykonos, as on all the Greek islands, is an important part of daily life. This fisherman *above* is preparing his nets and baskets beside the harbour; fishing boats lie at anchor *top right*. One of the famous pelicans waits patiently for a friend to turn on the water for a drink *far right*, and the most famous sight of all is the windmills, etched against a blue sky *right*. Only one still grinds wheat into flour, working as a tourist attraction; three others have been converted into charming houses while the remainder are falling into ruin. Mykonos is swept almost constantly during the summer months by a strong north wind, the meltemi, which buffets the boats in the harbour and tears at the tables and chairs on the waterfront. It is the meltemi, however, which keeps the otherwise unbearable heat at bay and gives Mykonos its invigorating climate and, of course, drives the windmills.

Delos, the Sacred Island, traditionally the birthplace of Apollo, is a tiny island in the Cyclades. It is reached by boat on day trips from Mykonos and is a treasure island of classical ruins *bottom left*, statues such as the famous Lions *left* and beautiful mosaics, all dedicated through the centuries to the great god Apollo.

Santorini *right and below* is a volcanic island in the south Aegean Sea. It is actually only half a volcano as the rest split away and sank into the sea during an eruption or an earthquake thousands of years ago. Ships land visitors inside what was the crater, and they climb the zigzagging road to the town riding on donkeys. The little town perches on the remaining rim of the crater. Recent excavations indicate that Santorini was once an important link between the Cretan or Minoan and the ancient Greek civilisations. Some believe it to be the remains of the lost Atlantis.

These three pictures encapsulate the charms and contrasts of the Greek islands as they are today, dominated by water, fishing, sunshine and ancient ruins. They show the town and the harbour of Karpathos in the Dodecanese Islands *above*, ruins at Ios *top right* and boats at Paros *right*. These last two islands are in the Cyclades.

Crete is the largest and most southerly of the Greek islands. Because of its shape and position it acts as a natural barrier to the Aegean islands and is of obvious strategic importance. The ancient civilisation which eventually spread all over Greece originated here. For about 1,500 years until the fourteenth century B.C. there was a powerful Minoan civilisation with its capital at Knossos; excavations have exposed the palace *top right and above.* There were many wall paintings in the palace but those we see today are largely Victorian restorations *left and far left* which probably bear little resemblance to the originals.

Crete is a mountainous island with snow-capped peaks and beautiful valleys but there are also sandy beaches like this one at Elunda, Aghios Nikolaos *top left.*

The island of Rhodes, the capital of the Dodecanese Islands, is strategically placed in the eastern Aegean Sea only twenty kilometres from the coast of Asia Minor. It owes its fame to Knights of St. John who, having been forced out of their stronghold in Jerusalem, eventually moved to Rhodes in 1309 and remained there for over 200 years. The fortified city of Rhodes which was built by the Knights can still be seen today almost as it was 500 years ago but there is also a modern town *below*. Mandraki harbour is used by cargo caiques and yachts. At the entrance *left* are two pillars surmounted by a stag and a doe, the emblems of Rhodes. St. Nicholas Fort which was built in 1464 can be seen in the background.

The lovely village of Lindos is built on the site of one of the three ancient Dorian cities of Rhodes. The present village dates from the fourteenth and fifteenth centuries and many of the mediaeval houses still survive *right*.

Overleaf: The Parthenon on the Acropolis, Athens.

First published in Great Britain 1978 by Colour Library International Ltd.
© Illustrations: CLI/Bruce Coleman Ltd. Colour separations by La Cromolito, Milan, Italy.
Display and text filmsetting by Focus Photoset, London, England.
Printed and bound by Group Poligrafici Calderara - Bologna - Italy
Published by Crescent Books, a division of Crown Publishers Inc.
All rights reserved.
Library of Congress Catalogue Card No. 77-94420
CRESCENT 1978